A Windy Day

A true tale of a tiny mouse adventure

Written & Illustrated by Cyndy Callog

Cyndy Callog LLC

PO Box 409
Pentwater, Michigan 49449
info@cyndycallog.com

cyndycallog.com

Printed by Friesens in Altona, Manitoba, Canada.

ISBN 978-0-692-79324-4

1. Mouse, birds, animals. 2. Nature art.
3. Human-animal relationships. 4. Conduct of life.
Non-fiction
Library of Congress Control Number: 2016917155

10 9 8 7 6 5 4 3 2 1

Callog, Cyndy
Windy Day, A
by Cyndy Callog
Illustrated by Cyndy Callog
Cyndy Callog LLC © 2017

Summary: A true story of an artist and her husband who rescue a baby mouse, and the special relationship and adventures they share.

Dedicated in loving memory
to my mother, Carolyn, and
to my aunt, Ellie.

The joy that Nitro brought to our lives . . .
which we shared with others . . .
to which we all opened our hearts . . .
resulted in smiles, wonder
and the writing of this book.

Our time spent with Nitro,
which we considered a gift,
becomes a story for those who
learn to listen and
act with their hearts —
as hearts understand
all languages
and respect all life.

Prologue

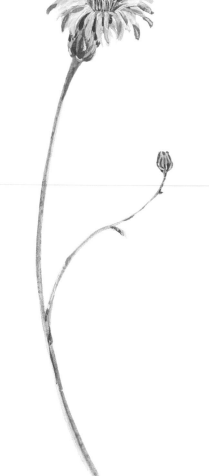

"*squeak!*

...errr...I mean, Hi!"

I'm Nitro, a legendary mouse in my mouse world! I'm brave, adventurous, and oh so fortunate to have been rescued by my human friends, George and Cyndy.

MY UNUSUAL TALE IS TRUE!

Our story has been told so many times that George, Cyndy and I have decided to write it all down for everyone! Cyndy painted all of the pictures. I sure am cute, aren't I?

It's such an awesome story. I can't wait to begin!

Watch for George's cap  which will mean that my George and Cyndy are telling their part of the story.

When you see my mouse tracks, you'll know it's me telling the same part of the story from my mouse point of view.

O.K., O.K. Here we go! A great mouse adventure is about to begin!

"*Yip!*
~*Yip!*"

The leaves were swirling all around on that windy day.

George had been walking down the path to work in the old barn that is part of our art studio.

"Oh no! I almost stepped on a baby mouse," George exclaimed as he quickly jumped aside. "What in the world are you doing out here all alone? The wind is going to whisk you away...or maybe that is how you got here?"

"Come look!" George shouted. "A baby mouse is sitting right in the middle of the path!"

Setting her work aside, Cyndy ran outside.

"Oh! How tiny.... It's no bigger than an acorn!"

The baby mouse was covered with grey fuzz. Its eyes were still closed. A slight whisker twitch was the only movement from the sad looking baby mouse.

"Let's leave the mouse here for awhile to see if the mother returns." However, Cyndy was quite worried.

Still wearing his work gloves, George gently lifted the tiny mouse to set him off the path, protected from the wind, in some leaves.

1

You've just read George and Cyndy telling their part of the beginning of our story.

Now you've found my mouse tracks, good! So you know I am telling you the same part of the story from my mouse point of view.

The beginning of my story is very sad. Before I start, I have something very important to say so you won't be too afraid. After all, I've grown to be a very wise mouse now.

"Sadness comes into every life, even that of a mouse. Happiness comes to every life too. With hope and courage, we can learn to find joy again in new ways."

Ahem. Excuse me while I clear my throat. O.K. O.K. I, Nitro, the storyteller mouse, am ready to begin.

My **day of great sadness** dawned like any other, all cozy and snuggled in my mouse house with my mouse family. My mom's soft chirps and chips were comforting. She was nuzzling and cleaning us while we fed.

All of a sudden, she gasped.

"NO! OH NO!"

Fear tore through my heart.

Terrible screeching and scuffling sounds whirled around me in the dark. My baby legs were too tiny to run. Somehow, with a horrible whoosh and a tumble, I was flung out onto the rough ground.

"Where are you, Mom? What happened? Oh Mom! Mom! Help me!!" I called and squeaked and cried into the oh-so-cold silence. Before I even had time to think, the stillness was broken by a heavy ka-thump!

"Yow! What was that?"

I felt a large shadow brush over me. It crunched right down by my toes. I couldn't move. I don't even think I was breathing, I was so frightened.

All was quiet for a few minutes until I was scooped up by a gentle warmth. My heart jumped!

"Mom! Oh Mom! Is that you?"

But no. I was alone, back on the ground, in some leaves. At least the wind was no longer swirling around me.

The windy autumn afternoon was becoming cooler. Each time Cyndy walked by, she so hoped the baby mouse would be back with its mother. Each time, it was still in the leaves.

"How hungry and cold the baby mouse must be by now," she talked with George. "Its little head is drooping lower. Its tiny nose is barely twitching anymore."

By now it was time to leave the studio to go home. Knowing they just couldn't abandon the poor little mouse, Cyndy hurried to find a box.

After tucking a soft cloth around the cold mouse, she held the box carefully in her lap as George drove them home.

The mouse drifted off to sleep while Cyndy and George quietly discussed what they were going

to

do

with a

mouse!

From the tip of my tiny nose to my tiny toes and all the way to the tip of my tail, I felt nothing but coldness. I could barely squeak as the voices and thumps gathered around me once more.

"Eeek, here I go again."

The same gentle warmth scooped me up, but this time set me down in something soft! I snuggled in.

Even though I didn't know where I was going and wasn't where I wanted to be, I was just so happy to be warm! My shivering soon stopped. Somehow I wasn't quite so afraid.

I began to understand that these must be the humans my mom talked about. She said some are nice and kind...I hoped these were.

Exhausted from its sad day, the baby mouse drifted off to sleep. The quiet voices continued talking.

It didn't take long for Cyndy and George to arrive home.

"Do you think it will be warm enough if I set the mouse box on a heating pad?" she asked.

"Yes, that will work, but we can't keep calling him 'the mouse'. We need a real name. He seems to be a tough little guy. How about Nitro?" George suggested.

Of course George liked a name like 'Nitro'. He raced a car called a dragster. Instead of regular gasoline, it used a fuel called Nitromethane, which made it go very fast.

"Our cats have race car names, so should the mouse," Cyndy agreed.

Hemi and Viper were wild kittens when they, too, were rescued by Cyndy and George. Hungry and lost, the small kittens were found in George's race car trailer.

"Hemi and Viper have grown up to be very good cats," Cyndy said proudly. "They only go outside when I do and I have taught them not to hurt any creatures." She was thinking Nitro would be happy to know this!

While they were getting Nitro settled with his new name, in his new mouse box, he woke up!

I slowly awoke from a sound sleep.

"Ahhh, I feel much better." As I stretched awake, there was a tiny, mouse-sized excitement growing within me.

"What will happen to me next?" I wondered while listening to the voices.

"So far, so good with these humans. They seem to be caring for me. I think their names are Cyndy and George."

"Hey! Wait a minute! What are they calling me? Nitro? It doesn't sound like Mom's name for me, but I like it."

Right then, another feeling came over me.

As the top of my box opened, I shouted in my loudest baby mouse squeak:

" Hello...
I'm
starving!!"

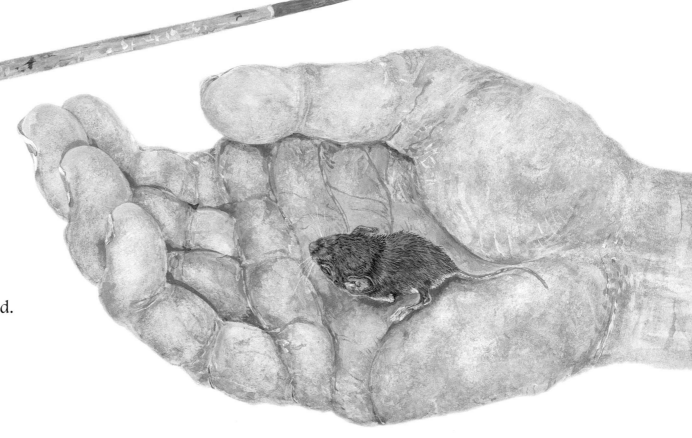

George was holding Nitro in his hand, while Cyndy was trying to feed him warm milk.

"We've tried everything! An eye dropper, dripping milk on your hand, but nothing is working!" She was concerned. "I know a baby mouse needs to be fed often."

"Tsst! Click!" They heard little mouse sounds. They could tell Nitro was upset. Too much milk was going up Nitro's tiny mouse nose.

George realized Nitro didn't know how to sip. "A baby would normally nurse from its mother."

"I have an idea!" Cyndy quickly went to get one of her small paint brushes. She brushed milk on George's palm in thin layers.

"It's working!" George cheered. "He's sipping the milk!"

"Nitro figured it out!" Cyndy marveled. "The brush is just what he needed!"

They both sighed in relief.

"*Tsst! ~Tsst!*
click! ~click!"

"Hey! I don't need a bath! I need to eat! Click!"

"Aah-choo! It's going up my nose! Click! Click!"

"O.K., humans, we have to work together here! I don't know whether to laugh or cry. Have either of you noticed my size and that my eyes are closed?"

"*Tsst!*
click!"

"*Yip! ~Yip!* What's this? It may be just right! I can do this!" I sipped eagerly.

"*Umm,*
this ~tastes
so ~good!"

The mouse slept well his first night with the humans. Cyndy and George did not, for they knew the baby mouse needed his milk every two hours. They didn't mind getting up to feed Nitro though, for he was trying so hard to survive.

Golden eyes and long white whiskers curiously watched over Nitro through the night also.

8

Mouse life and human life intermingled happily in the following days. Cyndy and George went shopping for an actual cage for Nitro, adding a cardboard tube.

They also bought mouse vitamins and experimented with other milks and baby formulas, but settled on warmed rich cream. Nitro loved it and did well.

"He knows us, doesn't he?" Cyndy was delighted.

"Yes, he trusts us," George reflected.

Whenever they called, "Nitro," the baby mouse would always pop right out of his cardboard tube to say hi, with friendly chips and squeaks.

One morning George and Cyndy were so surprised and excited. They couldn't believe their own eyes, for two tiny black eyes were twinkling back at them!

Nitro's eyes

were *wide* *open!*

One morning,
as I popped out of
my cardboard tube, about to
squeak "Hi," I was so
surprised and amazed!
"Wow!
I can see!"
I looked all around me, up and
down, inside and out.
"Oh! My humans!
Hi! This is
awesome!"

10

Nitro had just pulled his cardboard tube, full of paper, up to the upper level of his mouse house.

"You funny little mouse," Cyndy smiled. "Do you like your nest upstairs?"

Chewing, shredding and running on his new wheel, the young mouse was having a happy mouse childhood.

"Nitro," she coaxed. Nitro came right onto Cyndy's hand. Little Nitro wiggled all over in expectation. His tiny feet danced in her hand until he was happily sipping cream.

Cream first, then a quick circle around, and Nitro was ready for his mouse massage.

"I am amazed by how affectionate he is," Cyndy beamed.

Keeping his little mouse head flat on her palm, Nitro would stretch, close his eyes, roll on one side, then the other, all the while being rubbed.

"Which does Nitro like better, eating or his mouse massage?" George chuckled.

Often George and Cyndy's art business took them on trips out of town. Nitro couldn't be left alone since he still needed regular feedings of his cream, now mixed with oat cereal. Besides needing regular feedings, it was much too cold to leave the baby mouse in their car.

So, in his small green carrying bag, Nitro, such a well-behaved mouse, attended business meetings, went shopping, and slept in a Bed and Breakfast. He even sat in on (or under as it were!) a business lunch meeting.

"What would they say if they knew we had a mouse under the table, tucked in a bag with our business notes and papers?" Cyndy wondered.

"Some people would enjoy meeting him, some would screech," George offered. "I think it's best to be quiet as a mouse about this."

"I feel sorry for anyone who would screech at Nitro," she decided. "He would be happy to meet them."

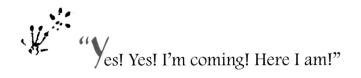 "Yes! Yes! I'm coming! Here I am!"

"Hurry! Hurry! Pick me up!"

"Oh! my most favorite time!"

"My Cyndy just called my name so I know it is time for warm cream and oat cereal. I'm glad she isn't ticklish because I'm so happy I can never stop wiggling! After all, as I said, it is my most favorite time."

"Ahhh, now this is the life," I thought as I circled around for my mouse massage. "My human friends are the best!"

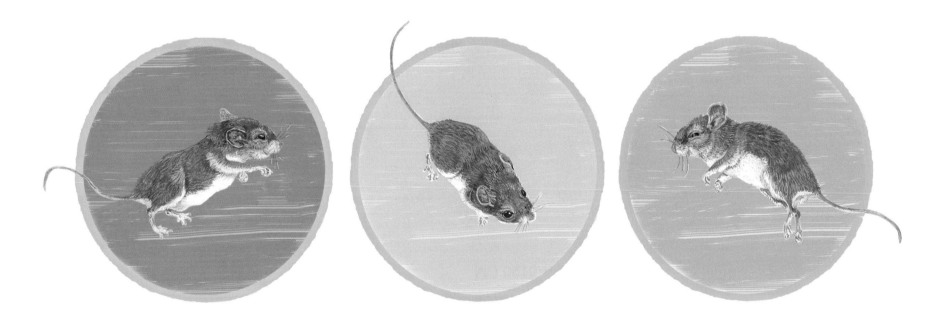

"I am now a 'mouse about town,' so I'm told!" chirped Nitro.
"I have spent many hours traveling, experiencing new smells, sounds, and sights."

Nitro decided that as long as he was with his humans, held often and fed well,
he was a very happy mouse.

"I love to hold this soft little mouse! Look how big his ears are! He's so cute!" Cyndy was half-talking to Nitro and half talking to George as she and Nitro were playing.

"Oh oh, wait a minute! George! Look! Something's wrong, he's losing his fur!"

"Come here, Nitro," he said as he gently took the little mouse.

"What's wrong with you?"

Bare patches of skin were beginning to appear all over the baby mouse.

"He must go to the vet," Cyndy insisted.

"I can't believe we're taking a wild mouse to the doctor," George grumbled. Shaking his head, he reached for the phone to make an appointment.

"Nitro trusts us to take care of him," she simply said.

Off to the vet they went.

Safe in his small green carrying bag, Nitro sat on Cyndy's lap at the Animal Hospital. A nervous Rottweiler was panting all over them.

"Nitro!" The nurse's loud voice echoed across the waiting room. All the other waiting people looked at the Rottweiler, thinking the big dog was surely named Nitro. Instead, Cyndy stood up and walked across the long room carrying her little bag of mouse! Everyone laughed!

The doctor thought Nitro was adorable, as she examined him carefully.

"Nitro has mites, which often come in cedar chips," she explained.

"You should only use shredded newspaper in his cage.

He will need a shot now, and another one in two weeks to completely stop the cycle of mites."

Weighing Nitro, the vet said, "I'm not sure I have a needle tiny enough for this cute little mouse."

She was able to find one and with that, Nitro had his first shot.

The little mouse's "tssts" and "clicks" left no doubt that he was upset!

On the way home, Cyndy informed Nitro about the mites and the shot, hoping he would understand that the pain was necessary.

"I can't believe you are giving a medical explanation to a baby mouse," George laughed fondly.

"Arrrgh! What is wrong with me?"

"I'm so itchy I can't even play. I have to scratch so much."

"My legs are exhausted from scratching my ears, then my stomach, next my sides, then everywhere all over again."

"By the way, my Cyndy, what was that comment about my big ears? Don't you know a wild mouse needs big ears to listen for danger?"

"Humph, you'd better say I'm cute!"

"Now why has she put me in my carrying bag? Where are we going?"

The trip was a short one and I soon found myself sitting next to the biggest nose I've ever seen!

"Phew! Dog breath!"

"Why is this guy so nervous? Has he been here before? He must know something I don't know."

ANIMAL HOSPITAL

"Nitro!" A loud voice called out.

"Yikes, who was that? Now I'm really worried!"

I repeated to myself, "My Cyndy is with me. I'm okay...I'm okay...I'm okay."

"Hee hee hee, someone's tickling me! It sure is cold and bright in here. I'd much rather be home. What is this all about anyway? They sure are talking a lot."

All of a sudden, something poked me.

"*Ouch!*"

"Enough of that," I squeaked in my sternest mouse voice.

"*Tsst! ~Tsst! Click! ~Click!*"

Nitro was rather grouchy on the way home. As Cyndy held and talked to him, the mouse relaxed and fell asleep, knowing everything was okay again. Sometime during his mouse nap, the itching stopped.

With his spoon and carton of ice cream, George was in treat heaven. Nitro was equally content sitting in Cyndy's lap, nibbling his new snacks.

The young mouse was finally eating on his own, enjoying a variety of seeds and grasses. Sunflower seeds, berries and millet were his favorites.

"He's outgrown his cream and grown into his ears," George noted. "Not only that, he is becoming nocturnal in his habits, isn't he?"

"I know, he's so active in the evening, so quick," Cyndy remarked.

"Come here, little guy," George was being tickled, as Nitro was now running up his arm! "If you're ready for playtime, it's back to your cage. You can safely run and jump all you'd like in your playground."

"He's still a sweet little mouse but I think he's becoming a teenager!" Cyndy lamented.

Later that evening, George heard a shout. He bounded upstairs.

"Help! Help! George! Open the door slowly!" she warned him. "Nitro just jumped out of my hands!" George went into the bedroom very carefully as Cyndy explained what happened.

"I was holding Nitro, saying goodnight to him as usual. The next second he flew out of my hands, bounced off the edge of the bed and flipped underneath. I dashed over to the door to put a rug up against the bottom gap so he couldn't escape the room. I don't think he even knew what he was doing! His little feet just jumped ahead of his brain."

"Well, at least he's still in this bedroom," George reasoned. "Let's leave his cage door open and see what he's up to in the morning. Goodnight, little mischievous mouse!"

"Ha! Ha! This is cool! Relaxing with my human friends! These new seed flavors are yum-yum good!"

"My George sure enjoys his ice cream. I've been trying to nibble as fast as he spoons, but now I'm full!"

"Ahhh," I stretched and yawned. "I believe, since I am indeed a satisfied and wide awake mouse right now, I will jump over to play with George."

"Let's see...I'll just slip under his cuff...ooh ha-ha...I'll tickle up his arm!"

"Surprise! Hee hee! Hi to you!" I squeaked with a mouse giggle!

I certainly was not really ready to go upstairs with George, but he took me back to my cage. While I busied myself with important mouse activities, tending to my nest and running in my wheel, I continued to feel restless? Curious? Impatient?

The beginnings of teenage mouse thoughts were stirring.

"Yip! Yip!"

"Whew, I just set a speed record for my running wheel," I gasped, panting to catch my breath.

"Oh! Here comes my Cyndy to say goodnight."

"Hello! Hello to you," I chipped happily, and into her hands I jumped...and a second later, I leaped out of her hands!

"Yeow! What have I done? Why did I do that?" My legs just kept running. I zipped under the bed.

"Now I'm really in trouble!" thought one part of my teenage mouse brain.

"Boy, this is fun!" thought the other part of my teenage mouse brain.

"I am sorry to disappoint my humans...but maybe I'll explore just for a little while...behind the chair...under the dresser...can I squeeze into a drawer?"

"Ha! Ha!"

Change, even in a mouse's life, is inevitable.

very so often Cyndy or George entered the bedroom to leave fresh water and seeds.

"Nitro, come here little mouse," they urged.

Soft squeaks, and wiggling and scratching noises would then be heard from inside the dresser. It was Nitro, just saying he was O.K. But for **the very first time ever,** no little mouse nose or eyes would peek out.

"Nitro is enjoying being independent way too much," Cyndy fretted.

"Yes, he is," George nodded. "We are going to have to catch him somehow. There are only two more days until his next vet appointment and his final mite shot."

"As sweet as he has been, he is a wild mouse," Cyndy sighed. Her voice was small and sad. "We will have to decide where to set him free."

The next morning, George removed the dresser drawers, one by one. Cyndy kept talking to Nitro, trying to persuade him.

"Nitro's been here for sure," she confirmed. "My favorite old velvet rabbit has been chewed into a mouse nest."

The dresser now stood empty of drawers with no mouse in sight.

George then looked more closely. There, perched on a wooden support ledge along the back of the dresser, sat the little mouse.

"Come here you cute mouse! You're being a little dickens, aren't you? We've missed you!"

Nitro tiptoed onto Cyndy's hand.

"I'm so sorry we have to return you to your cage," she comforted him. "Don't worry! It will only be for two more days. Then you will be free to be a grown-up, wild mouse."

I explored...through the whole night...all through the next day...into the following night...and into the second morning.

After investigating every nook and corner of the bedroom, I decided to make my new home in the tall dresser.

Can you guess where my nest was? It was in the top drawer, up high as usual. I found something very soft and snuggly, like velvet, which I shredded for my cozy nest.

Next, I scurried back and forth from my cage to the bottom dresser drawer—so many trips, I lost count! Moving all my seeds to my new home, piling them into four very neat mounds, left me a little tired but quite pleased.

Knowing Cyndy and George checked on me was reassuring. I probably should have peeked out, but I was so busy and so excited!

"Hello! Hello! I'm doing great. Thanks!" I squeaked instead.

Running and exploring throughout my new tall mouse house was so much fun.

My freedom ended the morning that George removed the fourth drawer.

"Hi, my Cyndy," I chipped with mixed emotions as I perched on the ledge.

I tiptoed onto Cyndy's hand...

I was happy because I had missed her...

I was embarrassed because of my unexpected, leaping escape...

I was reluctant because it had been very cool to be on my own.

"Hemi! Viper! Come for your treat," Cyndy called as she and George were getting ready for bed the next evening.

"Good girl, Viper, but where is Hemi?" she questioned.

It was very unusual for Hemi to miss his bedtime treat. A twinge of alarm flitted through her.

She glanced into the living room, but Cyndy knew that upstairs was where she needed to check quickly.

As she reached the top of the stairway, she was relieved to see that the door to Nitro's room was closed.

"Hem—!" Her call was cut short. Down the hallway, in a perfect cat crouch, Hemi was staring at the closet door. The twitching of his white whiskers and pink nose was the only movement belying his statue-like pose.

"What is it Hemi? Be gentle now," Cyndy said firmly, as she reached for the doorknob.

Two pairs of eyes peered into the closet just in time to see a flash of gray disappear into a narrow space behind a shelf.

"Oh no, don't tell me we have another mouse in our house," Cyndy gasped. She didn't know what to think! Nevertheless, she ran into Nitro's room to make sure he was safely inside his cage.

Nitro's cage was exactly the way she had left it in the afternoon, with the door tightly shut.

Except it was empty! There was no mouse!

"George! Nitro's escaped!"

George ran upstairs quickly.

"We'll set the mouse-size live trap this time." He calmly put some peanut butter in the trap.

"Hemi will keep track of him. Right now, we know Nitro's still in the closet."

"Nitro come back! Tomorrow we'll set you free. This is way too dangerous," pleaded Cyndy.

They could not believe that after all of their efforts, this mouse story would end with Nitro lost in the house.

"I don't want to be in a cage anymore. Excuse me! Humans! I thought you were my friends and cared about me. Can't you see I'm an independent mouse now?"

"I was having so much fun in my new tall mouse house. Come on! I was being careful and neat."

I was very upset. As my frustration grew, I ran faster and faster in my wheel. I made the wheel turn so fast that it flung me out onto the shredded paper. I did it over and over again.

Somewhere inside I knew that I should trust my George and Cyndy, but I did not stop to listen to my heart.

My anger had grown too big and it was too much in the way.

I was about to do something so very dangerous.

"They say if my nose fits, the rest of me will squeeze through.

I should not do this...I'm going to try... No...O.K., I'm going, here goes..."

I poked my nose out of the itty bitty extra space at the edge of the cage door.

Squisssch **Ooh~Ouch~Plop!**

"Ha! I'm out of here!"

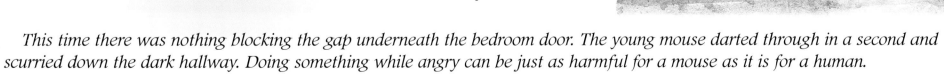

This time there was nothing blocking the gap underneath the bedroom door. The young mouse darted through in a second and scurried down the dark hallway. Doing something while angry can be just as harmful for a mouse as it is for a human.

Lying quietly in their bed, George and Cyndy's eyes were closed but their ears were wide open. Hemi was resting by their feet with his eyes closed, but his ears pointed straight down the hallway.

Snap!

Hemi leaped off the bed. They threw off the covers and followed Hemi. George opened the closet door to check the live trap.

"Oh no! We missed him."

"Come on, Nitro," Cyndy whispered, with her heart aching.

George re-set the live trap. They all assumed the same positions in bed. This time the wait was longer.

Finally! *Snap!*

Hemi leaped off the bed. Cyndy and George threw off the covers and followed Hemi. Cyndy was holding her breath as George opened the closet door.

"We have him!"

There was a safe, teenage mouse looking at them from inside the live trap.

"Oh you dear little mouse," Cyndy chided. "We were so worried about you. There's a great big wonderful mouse life ahead of you, but you almost lost it by your thoughtless behavior."

Her words ran together in her relief to have Nitro back, safe and sound.

"Come on little buddy." George carefully removed Nitro from the live trap. "I'm putting you in your original baby mouse cage. You won't be able to escape from that one."

"Sleep peacefully tonight, dear Nitro," Cyndy said, soothing him. "Tomorrow is your **truly exciting day,** the one you have been growing and learning...and longing for. It has nearly arrived."

Cyndy's worried~relieved~caring~sad~happy voice drifted in and out of my thoughts as George was taking me out of that snappy, scary, metal box. He rubbed me gently, then tucked me into my oh~so~small baby cage.

"This is a very difficult period of my life."

"I behaved poorly."

"I worried my human friends."

"I could have been hurt very badly. I love my Cyndy and George, but I think we all know it is time for me to be on my own."

I nestled under my cloth.

"I now will trust them to do what's best for me."

The subdued gray mouse slept peacefully.

22

The sun was warming that **very important** November morning. Cyndy named it the Bittersweet Day.

There was sadness in their hearts for they would no longer have Nitro with them.

The good feeling was that this is what should be happening. Nitro grew up well and now needed to be on his own to live the life intended for a wild mouse.

George and Cyndy finalized their plans to set Nitro free. Their first stop was the Animal Hospital.

"You have good mouse instincts and skills. Use them well," stated the veterinarian as she gave Nitro his second mite shot.
"You are healthy now. Enjoy your life in the big world!"
She still thought Nitro was the cutest mouse.

Cyndy and George had decided to release Nitro at their good friend Karen's farm. Her large old barn was full of alfalfa for her horses. This would provide food and shelter for the mouse.
There will be other mice for Nitro to meet too, she thought as they slowly approached the farm, turned down the bumpy driveway, and stopped.

I awoke with a tingling inside, a **very important excitement.**

"I know I am hungry, but this feels different. What was Cyndy saying, that I'm finally a grown-up mouse?"

"How did I ever fit in this baby cage? Was I really so tiny once?"

I nibbled seeds but mostly I lay quietly, reflecting on my experience and lessons from last night, waiting...

"Well, we're off! Where could we be going?" I wondered with an anxious mouse wonder. In the back of my mind, the words, 'mite shot' were flitting around.

I was right—and not at all happy.

"Not this cold-bright-tickly room again!"

" *Ouch! —Tsst! —click! —click!*"

"Did she say I'm still the cutest? Ahhh...!"

"Enough of this! O.K., what's next?"

I knew there was something else. Cyndy was holding me in her hands as we resumed traveling. I held quite still since I could sense she was quite tense. I sure was too!

A short time later, the car slowed, turned, bumped along a bit and finally stopped. *I sat up!*

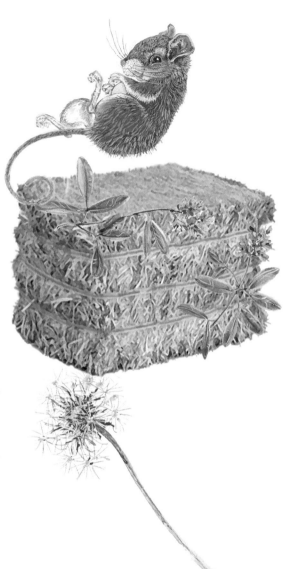

Geörge put Nitro in his jacket pocket and zipped it closed. Cyndy took some sunflower seeds with her, to leave for Nitro.

The huge wooden door rolled back with a slow creak. As they entered, the beautiful horses perked their ears forward. Gentle nickers greeted them, as well as the sweet smell of alfalfa. Cyndy began to cry.

"Don't be too sad, he'll do very well here," George assured her.

"I know, I do want him to be happy. I will just really miss him."

"So will I."

George climbed up onto a bale of alfalfa. He could feel the little mouse wiggling in his pocket.

"O.K.! O.K.! Come on little buddy!" After a few rubs behind Nitro's ears, George set him down onto the bale.

Nitro lifted his feet in hesitant steps, tried many running steps, followed by several leaps in the air! He circled the many bales to come right back to sit in front of George and Cyndy.

George rubbed Nitro's chin.

Through her tears, Cyndy encouraged, "It's O.K. Go now, be a great mouse!"

Nitro sat with them for a few more moments.

The time had come. Nitro turned and with a couple more dancing leaps, disappeared into a small opening between the bales.

George was laughing, "Wow."

Joy overcame Cyndy's tears.

"He actually said good-bye to us."

They walked out of the old barn, hand in hand.

"Why are you putting me in your jacket pocket, George? It's so dark and stuffy!"

Only one "tsst" escaped through my whiskers, for I knew to trust my George and Cyndy. Something big was about to happen, even though I couldn't see a thing.

"What do I hear? Is Cyndy saying...horses?
Hello to you, ones who nicker and whinny!"

I was trying so hard to be good and patient. "What if George has forgotten about me?"
"Squuick!" It was a rather muffled squeak! "I'd better wiggle too, in case he didn't hear me."

The zipper opened. I peeked out. In a blink, without a doubt...

"This is it, the big world, where I need to be."

George set me down onto something oh so sweet smelling... alfalfa he called it.
My first steps were hesitant.
I looked up at my George and Cyndy.

"Are you sure? Is it O.K.?"

"Yippee!" I ran in a great big circle over the bales, adding several exuberant leaps, to sit right back in front of them.

I was very sad...I was very happy...

"Oh, don't cry, my Cyndy,
I will be a great mouse! Thank you!"

"Bye bye! Yip yip!"

With a couple more dancing leaps and a wave of his tail, Nitro, the grown up mouse, full of wisdom, health, confidence and love, dashed off on his own, to continue his special mouse life!

The End

of

THIS story

Use your knowledge and imagination to write the future chapters of Nitro's life . . .
Use your dreams to write the future chapters of your life . . .

You are the author of your own unique and wonderful story!

Author's note

The value in this story is that it reminds us of our continuity, awakening us to our connection with all living creatures.

Every life is more complex and beautiful than we often realize.

Every one of our actions affects all living things—therefore the need for responsible ones.

Serendipity moments, unexplained encounters, spiritual moments of lives shared—relationships between species do exist. Many stories have been told about pets and wild animals who have shared a deep bond with humans.

Hemi was one of these. As our vet said, he came to us on a different plane, another level, one of deep awareness and understanding. Never, for a moment, did we think that he would hurt Nitro.

All animals, when experienced as an individual, are who they are—a personality is evident.

Nitro was a joy. Always interested and interactive, snuggly, fun and so funny!

Unfortunately, mice are often considered pests. However, their purpose in the wild is very important. And you just read all that we learned about a mouse by saving its life.

By taking the time to recognize the value of life, even that of a little mouse, our lives were enriched.

Thank you

For the preparation and accomplishment of this book,

my heartfelt thanks goes to Barbara, for her love and fine secretarial skills;

to an exceptional team at Vada Color for their guidance and hard work;

to Karen McDiarmid, graphic designer and editor,

who's caring heart and talent are reflected in all she touches;

to Dick Schinkel, who's twinkle and kind encouragement

have supported me since the day I met him;

to my sharp and thoughtful readers, especially Kittie and Penny;

to artist Frederick C. Schmidt for the inclusion of his

super watercolor painting of George's dragster;

and to all of our family, friends and acquaintances for their smiles,

as we told and retold stories about our dear little Nitro.